NUTAUI'S CAP

NUTAUI UTAKUNISHKUEUN

NUTAUI'S CAP

NUTAUN UTAKUNISHKUEUN

text by Bob Bartel

artwork by
Mary Ann Penashue

Translated by
Stella Rich, Sebastian Piwas,
and Mani Katinen Nuna
with Laurel Anne Hasler,
Penash Rich,
and Marguerite MacKenzie

Mani Katinenipan Nuna,
ka kukuminashiut, ka umishimaut,
ka ukaumaut, ka ukumimaut, ka anishkutapeut,
ka nakatuenitak innu-tipenitamuna,
ka shutshishiteieshkumit ute nutenaminat

For the late Mani Katnen Nuna,
elder, older sister,
mother, grandmother, great grandmother,
protector of Innu rights,
heart of our community

Photo credit: Bob Bartel

The Labrador Innu speak two dialects
of their language Innu-aimun.
In this text the Sheshatshiu dialect is presented first,
followed by the English
and finally the Mushuau dialect.

"Tshika tshi uitsheutin a natshi-kusseini, Nuta ? Ehe a ?"

Ninanatuapaten nikushkan kie nikushkaniapi ka-titipapitshepanua nekanissit. "Shash nishupishimua ute nititanan, kie nin kuessipan nika ui katshitinau namesh."

"Can I go fishing with you, Nuta? Can I?"

I scrambled for the fishing gear, the hook and line wrapped around a Carnation milk tin. "We've been here two months and it's my turn to catch a namesh."

"Tshika tshi a uitsheutin natshi-kusseni, Nuta ?"

Kuet natuapataman nikusseu-apatshitauna, titipinatshishtakanu tshitshinapunat nisheku-unakanitsh. "Tshash nishupishimua tshititaiai, eku kuessiman nipa ui nipaiau namesh.

"Shash tshikutunnuepipuneshin, Nanass," nititik[u] nutaui. "Innu kassinu ishinakuannu tshetshi nitau-kusset."

Nikuashkuepaniun anite tshishtapakunit ekue unuitaik nutaui. Nutaui nashkuepitam[u] ka uasheshkunanit tshiashi-utakunishkueun. Innu uepashtashun ashpikuatakanu anite utakunishkueunit, ui uapatiniueu anite uetshit.

"You're ten years old, Nanass," Nutaui said. "It's time. Every Innu needs to learn to fish."

I bounced on the fir boughs that made up the tent's floor, then pulled Nutaui through the doorway. Nutaui grabbed his well-worn blue Innu Nation ball cap on the way out. The Innu flag on the front showed the world where he belonged.

"Tshash tshipeikunnu-tatupipuneshin, Nanass," nititik[u] nutaun. "Muk[u] eshinakushit innu tshika tshishkutamuakanu tshetshi kusset."

Nikuashkuashkuepaniun anita ashititsh kuet ueuetak anite ueuetimitsh. Nutaun nashkuepitam[u] utakunishkueun ka uasheshkuianitsh. Innu Nation uepashtashunnu tshikamunu anita utakunishkueunitsh. Ui uapatiniueu utassin anite uetshit.

Nishatshinissetaiau, nipitshepimipatashin anite nutaui ushakameshimit. Mishta-nutishu anite e niuashit nipi, apu shatshimeushkat.

Anite nitapinan ashinit, nutaui nitshishkutamak^u tshe ishi-kusseiakatamuk mak tshe ishi-uepinikusseuk.

Shash ekue nutatam^u namesh.

"Mitshimin, metikat utin," nititik^u nutaui. Mishta-aiatshipaniu namesh, nitakuananan. Nipakuaten tshetshi uitamukau nikaui mak nukum.

Burying my hand in his strong grip, I skipped to Nutaui's favourite fishing spot, where shallow water curled around rocks and wind blew away black flies.

Sitting on a large rock at river's edge, Nutaui taught me to bait the hook, cast the line, and bring it in.

A namesh soon took the bait.

"Hang on, bring it in slowly," Nutaui encouraged. The namesh fought hard, but we reeled it in. I wanted to run and tell Nikaui and Nukum right away.

Nimakunamuai utitshin kuet uinipunan anite nutaun kushkapitsh. Niuashu mak mitsheia ashinina, mishta-nutin uepashuatsh pikushatsh.

Nitetapinai mishapishkau ashinin anita shipitsh, kuet nutaun tshishkutamuk tshetshi kusseiakataman nikushkannu, mak tshetshi uepinaman nikushkan kuet minuatsh utshipitaman.

Namesh mutatam^u nikushkannu.

"Kapita akuan," nititik^u nutaun. Mishta-shutshishiu namesh, muk^u nitakuashitatshimaiai. Tshinishtipa nui uitamuautsh nikaun mak nukum.

"Uinishtam tshika ui nashkumau Missinak^u mianitak^u namesha," nititik^u nutaui.

    Katshi nashkumuian, nitapishikuashkuau, ekue tshiuetaik.

    "Apu tshika ut pakashtuepaniun minuat," nititau ninameshim, "tshika mukaun."

    Ekue papit nutaui.

"First, you must give thanks to Missinak^u, the Water Spirit, for giving us the namesh," Nutaui said.

    After giving thanks, Nutaui and I hooked the slippery namesh to a stick and carried it to camp.

    "You're not getting away," I said. "You're invited for supper."

    Nutaui laughed.

"Nishtam tshika ui nashkumau Missinak^u katshi ashu-minitak^u namesha," nititik^u nutaun.

    Katshi nashkumunan, nitapishikuashkutshimau kuet tshiuetatshitsh anite nitshinatsh.

    "Mauatsh minuatsh tshika tshi pakashtuepaniun," nititau namesh. "Tshika uitshishpuminai."

    Papu nutaun.

"Nika, uapam ninameshim ka nipaik," nititau nikaui piatutsheian.

"Tshitshue mishta-mishishtu tshinameshim," issishueu nikaui, ekue ushameshet. Nitishpitenimikuat nikaui mak nukum. "Nika mumeshenan mak nika muanan innu-pakueshikan."

Uikanisha uashkapuat anite kutuanit. Uitshimakushaueu namesh anite ishkutet peminuenanuti. Nin an ninameshim ekue etatu ashamikauian. Mishta-uitshitu.

"Look what I caught, Nika!" I shouted, entering the tent.

"It's an enormous namesh," Nikaui said proudly as she and Nukum prepared our meal. "I guess we'll be having namesh and pakueshikan."

The family sat around the crackling campfire. Smells of frying fish and burning wood filled the air. It was my namesh, so I ate extra. It tasted delicious.

"Nika, uapamima namesh nepak !" nimishta-aiashikuei eti-pitsheian innutshuapitsh.

"Mishta-mishitu tapue tshinameshim," nititik^u nikaun kuet ushameshet. Nitishpitenimikuatsh nikaun mak nukum. "Nika mumesheiai mak nika muauiai pakueshikai."

Unitshinikua uashkapuatsh anita kuetuetsh. Uitshimakushu namesh peminuanitsh mak uitshimakuan anite ueuetimitsh. Nin ninameshim, nin nimishta-muau. Tshitshue mishta-uitshitu.

Nukum tipatutam^u nitassinan. Nutaui tipatuteu mashkua, nishka mak atikua.

Shassikut mishta-tshisheuepanu ekue kutaukauiat, mak iat nutaui. Tshisheuepanu nitei, nasht nipeten nishkassikanit. Minuat petueuepanu. Nitashikuen ekue pitutepataian anite patshuianitshuapit. Ninashakuat nikaui mak nukum.

"Katshishipanishiht an," nititik^u nikaui, ekue ueutshinit, shetshiku kie uin nikaui.

Nukum told stories of our land we call Nitassinan. Nutaui spoke of mashk^u, nishk and especially atik^u.

Without warning, a deafening boom drove us to the ground, even Nutaui. I heard my heart pound hard against my chest. Seconds later another ear-splitting blast struck us. I screamed and ran to hide in the tent. Nikaui and Nukum ran after me.

"It's the jets," Nikaui said holding me tight, her eyes showing her fear.

Nukum nitipatshimushtakunai nitassinatsh. Nutaun nitipatshimushtakunai mashkua, nishka mak atikua.

Shassikutsh mishta-tshisheuepanu tshekuan kuet nikapaniuiatsh anite assitsh. Tshishipanu niten anita nishkassikanitsh. Minuatsh pimueuepanu. Nitashikuei, nipishtepatai patshuianitshuapitsh. Nikaun mak nukum nuitshipatamikuatsh.

"Katshishipanishitsh," niteu nikaun. Nueuetshipitik^u, uashteiapitiku, shetshiniku.

"Nasht tapatakushuat," nititau, "tshekat tatshishinuat anite mishtikut.
Aueshishat kie uinuau kushtatshimikutshenat."

"Tan tshipa itinanapan innu-utit taiakuakue ?" issishueu nikaui.

Nitshitapamau nutaui. Mishta-tshishuaiku, mishta-makunitsheuiu.

"Nasht apu minuat," issishueu nutaui. "Nasht apu natutatak^u tshishe-
utshimau. Katshishipanishiht tshishkutamatishuat tshetshi patshitinahk
kapakapanissa ute tshitassinat. Ute Minai-nipit ka-tshititananua ekute
tekuannit tshetshi tshishkutamatishuht. Nasht tsheshka nitaiminan. Eshk^u iat
tshika pimipanuat.

"Kushtikuan ute. Tshika naunashunan."

"They were so low," I said, "they almost touched the trees. The animals must be
afraid too."

"What if we were in a canoe?" Nikaui worried.

I looked at Nutaui. He was muttering, his fists clenched tightly.

"This isn't right," Nutaui said. "The government won't listen. They want jets
to practice bombing over our land. This campsite in Minai-nipi is inside their
bombing range! Talking to them is useless. These flights will continue.

"It isn't safe here. We're packing up."

"Nasht tapatakushuatsh," nititau, "tshekat tatshishinuatsh anita mishtikutsh. Aueshishatsh kie kushtatshimikutshenitshi."

"Tan tshipa tutakanaiatsh anite pimishkaiakuakue ?" mishimenitamishkaku nikaun.

Nitshitapamau nutaun. Aiashtunepanu, mishta-makunitsheuiu utitshin.

"Ama minuau," nissishueu nutaun. "Tshishe-utshimau ama natutam^{u}. Katshishipanishitsh tshishkutamashuatsh anite tshetshi patshitinatsh kapakapanitshi anite tshitassinatsh. Ute Minai-nipitsh ka-tshititaiaiaua, ekute tekuannitsh tshetshi tshishkutamashuatsh. Nasht tsheshka animuekatuakanitshenitshi. Eshk^{u} iapitsh tshika pimipanuatsh.

"Kushtikuan ute. Nika naunashunai."

Nikunenan nitshinana ekue tshiueiat anite Sheshatshit.

Nutaui uishameu nutim tshishennua tshetshi mamuituht. Katshi tshishi-utshimau-aiminanut, tekushinit nutaui. Nitshissenimau apu minuenitak.

"Tshekuan inanu ?" nititau nutaui.

"Kanata nasht apu natutatak[u]. Nika pimutenan anite tueunanit tshetshi eka pimipaniht katshishipanishiht," nititik[u] nutaui.

We broke camp and headed back to our village, Sheshatshiu.

Nutaui called a meeting of all the Innu elders. After the meeting Nutaui came home. His face was serious.

"What did you decide?' I asked him.

"Canada is not listening to us. We will walk on the airport runway so the jets will not fly," Nutaui said.

Nikuneiai nitshinaia kuet tshiueiatsh anite Sheshatshitsh.

Nutaun uishameu mishue tshishennua tshetshi aianimuanitsh. Katshi aianimuanitsh nutaun takushinu anite nitshinatsh. Tshishunakushu.

"Tan tshe itinatsh ?" nititau.

"Kanata ama tshinatutakunai. Nika pimuteiai anite kapiminashitsh ka tueutshi kie mauatsh tshika pimipanuatsh katshishipanishitsh," nititik[u] nutaun.

"Tshika uitsheutinau ma ?" nikuetshimau nutaui.

"Nutim auen, tshishennu mak auass, tshika pimuteu," nititik^{u} nutaui. "Tshika ui nakatuenitenan tshitassinan mak aueshishat anite nikan.

Shash uetitshipanit, nutim innuat mak nin nishaputuetenan mak nipashituepaniunan atatsheikanit. Nitshipishkuananat katshishipanishiht. Kamakunueshiht nipushikunanat puassa ekue tshitishitatshimimiht. Minuat ekue tekushiniat. Mitshetuau ninimashkuaitshenan, nipimutenan anite tueunanit mak nikushtinananat tshetshi upauht katshishipanishiht.

"Can I come too?" I asked.

"The young and the old must all walk," Nutaui said. "We must protect our future, our land and animals."

When the time came, whole families, old and young, including me, walked through gates and crawled over metal fences. We grounded the jets. Police took us off the runway in buses. But we came back. Again, and again, we gathered, walked on the runways, and stopped the jets.

"Nipa tshi a petutei kie nin ?" nikuetshimau.

"Ussinitshishuatsh mak ussinitshishkueuatsh mak tshishennuatsh tshipa pimuteuatsh," nititik^{u} nutaun. "Tshika ui tshishpeuateiai tshitassinu mak aueshishatsh."

Tshash utitshipanu, mishue innuatsh mak nin nipitsheiai mak nishakatshueiai atatshenikanitsh. Nikushtinaiatsh tshetshi upautsh katshishipanishitsh. Kamakunueshitsh nimanitatshimikunaiatsh anita puassitsh.

Muk^u minuatsh nitakushinai. Minuatsh nimamuinai, tshetshi pimuteiatsh anite kapiminashitsh ka tueutshi mak nikushtinaiatsh tshetshi upautsh katshishipanishitsh.

Peikutshishikua nikanishinanat mak nuitsheuakananat manukashuat anite tueunanit.

"Nanass, tshukumish Enik tshimikaim[u] apashuia mak manashteu tshetshi manukashuiat," nititik[u] nutaui. "Peshut tshishtapakunat tshetshi anasseian kie nin nika tshimatan patshuianitshuap."

Tetaut tshimatau nutaui katshishapissiteshinit tshetshi piminuenanut mak tshetshi tshishitet.

One day, the Innu, our family and friends, set up a protest camp at the end of the runway.

"Nanass, Uncle Enik is cutting trees for tent posts and gathering boughs," Nutaui said. "Bring boughs for the floor. I'll set up the canvas tent."

In the centre of the tent, Nutaui put a wood stove to cook and keep the tent toasty warm.

Eshk[u] anite patush, tshematatsh innutshuapa anite kapiminashinitshi ka tueunitshi.

"Nanass, tshukumish Enik tshimikaueu mishtikua tshe apatshitat anite innutshuapitsh mak maiashiteu," nititik[u] nutaun. "Pitukanatsh ashitatsh. Nika tshimatai innutshuap."

Tetautsh tshimatau nutaun katshishapissiteshinitsh. Ekuta tshe piminuanitsh mak tshetshi tshishitetsh.

Nukum nuapatinik^u tshe ishi-anasseuk.

"Ekute ute nimaushutan inniminana eshk^u eka tshimatakanit tueunan," nititik^u nukum.

Katshi manukashuiat, papaituat kamakunueshiht ekue itikauiat, "Akua tuta. Shimakanishat shatuapekashtauat assikumaniapi anite akau atatsheikanit. Auassat tshipa tshi pishtishuat."

Nukum showed me how to weave boughs for the floor.

"We picked blueberries here before they built the airport," she said.

After we pitched our tents, police came and said, "Be careful. The army rolled razor wire behind the wooden fence. Children could cut themselves."

Nukum nuapatinik^u tshe nishi-aiasseian.

"Ekute ute nimushunaiapan eshk^u eka takuatsh kapiminashitsh ka tueutshi," nititik^u nukum.

Katshi manukashunatsh, kuet takushinitsh kamakunueshitsh mak nitikunaiatsh, "Iakua anite. Shimakanishatsh shatuapekashtauatsh kakashiminisht-nishekuiapinu kueshtetshe atatshenikanitsh. Auassatsh tshipa tshi pishtishuatsh."

Nuitsheuakanat mak nin ninatshi-uapatenan assikumaniapi anite atatsheikanit. Nitshimushapinan anite papashtakua. Assikumaniapi pimapekashteu anite eshkuapekak atatsheikanit. Shateiapishtepanu anite ka tshinapishkat assikumaniapi ekue shetshikuian.

"Innuat tshika tshissenitamuat tshe tutahk," nitissishuen tshimut.

My friends and I went to the tall wooden fence to see the razor wire. We peered between planks. The razor wire stretched across the entire length of the fence. The sun flashing off razor tips frightened me.

"My people will find a way," I said softly.

Nuitsheuakaiatsh ninatshi-uapateiai anite kakashiminisht-nishekuiapin anite atatshenikanitsh. Tshimut ninakatuapamaiaiatsh anite atatshenikanitsh. Kakashiminisht-nishekuiapin pimapekashteu anita eshkuapekatsh atatshenikan. Shateiapassipanu anita kakashiminisht-nishekuiapin kuet tshitshue nishetshishin.

"Nitshinnuatsh tshika nanatu-tshissenitamuatsh," tshimut nitaianimuei.

Katshi tshetshishepaushinit, nukumish
Enik mak uitsheuakana manipiteuat
papashtakua anite ka tshikamuniti
atatsheikanit ekue akunahk
assikumaniapia tshetshi pimutenanut.
Tshishennuat, ukaumauat, utaumauat
mak utauassimuaua shaputueteuat
anite atatsheikanit, anite takusseuat
papashtakut ekue ituteht anite
tueunanit. Nitakunamuan nituss Puna
utitshi ekue pimuteiat papashtakut.

"Mishta-innishuat innuat mak apu
kushtatshiht," nititau.

Papikuenu nituss mak
nanamishkuenu.

Next morning, Uncle Enik and his friends pulled boards off the fence and placed them over the razor wire, making it safe to cross. The elders, mothers, fathers, and families walked through the hole in the fence, over the boards, and safely onto the runway. I held my aunt Puna's hand, as we carefully stepped across the boards.

"Innu are smart and brave, aren't we?" I said.

Aunt Puna smiled and nodded.

Minuatsh tshinetshishepapatsh nukumish Enik mak uitsheuakaia manipiteuatsh papatshitakua anita ka tshikamunitshi atatshenikanitsh kuet patashtaimuatsh kakashiminisht-nishekuiapin tshetshi pimuteiatsh. Tshishennuatsh, ukaumauatsh, utaumauatsh mak auassatsh pitsheuatsh anite atatshenikanitsh, anite takusseuatsh papatshitakutsh kuet pimutetsh kapiminashitsh ka tueunitshi. Nitakunamuai nituss Puna utitshin kuet pemuteiatsh papatshitakutsh.

"Mishta-matinenitamuatsh innuatsh mak ama kushtatshuatsh," nititau.

Papikuenu nituss Puna mak naiamishkuenu.

Anita pemuteiat tueunanit, shimakanishat upuassimuaua nitshitinikunanat.
Natshipanua puassa, kamakunueshiht iamiut ekue pushikuiat puassit.

    "Apu tapuetakanit tshetshi pitutshenanut ute ! Kanata tshishe-utshimau
utassi !" nitishi-tepuatikunanat kamakunueshiht.

    "Ninan au nitassinan !" iteu nutaui.

As we walked on the runway, military buses rushed to meet us. The buses
braked, police got off and ushered us on board.

    "You are trespassing! This is Canadian Military property!" the policeman
shouted.

    "This is Nitassinan, our homeland," Nutaui reminded him.

Anita pemuteiatsh kapiminashitsh ka tueutshi, shimakanishatsh upuassinu
tshitshitshinikunaiatsh. Puassa natshipanua, kamakunueshitsh amiuatsh
kuet pushinikunatsh puassitsh.

    "Ama tapuetakanu ! Kanata tshishe-utshimau utassin !" nitashikuatikunai
kamakunuesht.

    "Ninan nitassinan," tshissiumiku nutaun.

Ninashauau nituss pushit puassinu kie nitshitapamau kuishk^u kapimipanitasht.

"Innu-assi ume, namaieu tshin tshitassi, muk^u niminueniten katshi takushipatain," nititau. "Nitaieshkushiten tshitshue. Tshitshue katak^u nipimutenan tueunanit."

Nutim auen papu, kie kapimipanitasht. Puassa nitishitatshimikunan anite uiatshinanut.

I followed my aunt onto the bus and looked the bus driver in the eye.

"This is Innu land, not yours, but I'm glad you came," I said. "My feet are tired. We walked such a LOOOONG way on this runway."

Everyone laughed, even the bus driver. The buses brought us back to the runway camp.

Nitati-uitsheuau nituss eti-pitsheiatsh puassitsh, kuet kushkunnu nitshitapamau anite ussishikutsh kapimipanitasht.

"Innu-assin ute, namaieu tshin tshitassin, muk^u niminuenitei katshi takushipatain," nititau. "Nitaieshkushtetei. Tshitshue uaiu nipimuteiai kapiminashitsh ka tueutshi."

Mishue papinanu, mak kapimipanitasht papu. Nitshiuetatshimikunai anite ka uitshinatsh.

Uetakussit, nukum nitipatshimushtak^u anite utat ka papamishkat ute nitassinat, ekue petueuepanitshi kamakunueshiutapana mak puassa nitshinat. Mishta-tshishuapuat kamakunueshiht mak tshikaueuat.

Nunuitatshimunan anite nitshinat. Nikushtatshin, ekue utinamuk nutaui utitshi. Kamakunueshiht tepuateuat innu-utshimaua utishinikashunnu. Ekue nataht napeuat mak ishkueuat, ekue makunititshepitakaniht.

Tepuatakanu nutaui.

That evening, while Nukum told me about her long canoe trips through Nitassinan, police cars and buses roared to the camp's edge. The police were angry and loud.

We crawled out of the tent. Frightened, I found Nutaui's hand. The police barked names of leaders. As they walked to the front, the men and women were handcuffed.

Nutaui's name was called.

Eti-utakussitsh, nukum nitipatshimushtak^u anite utatsh ka papamishkatsh ute nitassinatsh, kuet petueuepatamakaia kamakunueshiutapaia mak puassa ute nitshinatsh. Mishta-tshishuapuatsh tshitshue kamakunueshitsh, mishta-aiashikueuatsh.

Nueuetatshimunai. Nishetshishin mak nitakunamuai nutaun utitshin. Kamakunueshitsh tepueuatsh innu-utshimauatsh utishinikashunuaua. Kuet natatsh napeuatsh mak nishkueuatsh, kuet makupitakanitsh.

Nutaun tepuatakanu.

"Matshi natime tshituss," nititik[u] nutaui. Niman, nitapuetuau nutaui, mak nitshitapamauat kamakunueshiht miakunaht nutaui.

   "Tshekuannu uet utinakanit nutaui ?" Nitshishuapin mak nikushtatshin.

   Natshinakanu nutaui anite kamakunueshiutapanit, ekue patshititat utakunishkueun anite assit.

"Go see your aunt," Nutaui said. Crying, I obeyed, and watched the police arrest him.

   "Why are they taking Nutaui away?" I was angry and frightened.

   As the officers crammed Nutaui into the police car, his Innu Nation ball cap fell into the dirt.

"Matshi natuapame tshituss," nititik[u] nutaun. Nimai, nitapuetuau nutaun, mak ninakatuapamauatsh kamakunueshitsh minakunatsh.

   "Tshekuannu uitsh utinatsh nutaun ?" Tshitshue nitshishuapin mak nishetshishin.

   Nashinakanu nutaun anite kamakunueshiutapanitsh, kuet utakunishkueun patshitat anite assitsh.

Ekue tshitshipaituht kamakunueshiht. Nitshitinamuan utakunishkueun ekue naikamuk nenu innu-uepashtashun ka ishinakuannit. Nitussat, Puna mak Manimat, nitshiuetaikuat.

"Anitshenat innuat ka makunakaniht tshika makunakanuat anite katak[u]," nititik[u] Manimat.

"Nanitam tshika mashikenan," issishueu.

The police sped away. I ran to pick up the cap and brushed the dirt off the flag. My aunts, Puna and Manimat, took me home for the night.

Aunt Manimat told me the people arrested would be taken to jail far away.

"We will always keep fighting," she said.

Kuet tshitshipanitutsh kamakunueshitsh. Nitshitinamuai nutaun utakunishkueun, kuet papuashtataian. Nitussatsh Puna mak Manimat nitshiuetanikuatsh.

Manimat nititik[u] innuatsh ka makunakanitsh tshika pushiakanuatsh anite uaiu.

"Mushinau ninutshikashunai," nititik[u] nituss.

Nasht nitakunamuan nutaui utakunishkueun nepaian. Nipuamun nutshimit ka-nitanaua. Nipuamutamuan nutaui ukutuan kie eshimakuak minashkuat. Niminamau kanataut kie kakussesht anite nepaian innutshuapit mak ninakatuenimikuht. Nipeten shipu.

"Ui shutshishi, Nanass," ka-nititikua shipu, "Nanitam innu tshika tipenitam[u] tshitassinan."

At night, I slept with Nutaui's cap. I held it close. In my dreams, I was back in the country. I smelled Nutaui, campfires, and forests. I smelled a hunter and a fisherman sleeping near me on the fir boughs of our tent, keeping me safe. I could hear the river.

"Be strong, Nanass," the river murmured. "Nitassinan will always belong to the Innu."

Nasht nitakunamuai nutaun utakunishkueun ishkanitipishkaua. Nipuatei nutshimitsh ka taian. Nipuatamuai nutaun ukutuan kie eshimakuatsh ute minashkuatsh. Nimishimamau kanatuiut kie kakussesht anite nepaian innutshuapitsh mak ninakatuenimikuatsh. Nipetei shipu etueuekutsh.

"Ui shutshishi, Nanass," ka-nitikua shipu, "Innu mushinau tshika nakatuenimiku utassin."

NUTAUI'S CAP

Backgrounder

The Innu people inhabit Nitassinan, their word for "Our Homeland." Nitassinan is a vast area of boreal forests, lakes, rivers, and barrens that spans much of Labrador and Eastern Quebec. Innu elders say Innu have inhabited this land since the beginning of time. They know this from their oral tradition—stories passed on from one generation to the next. Artifacts found by archaeologists reveal that the Innu lived on this land as far back as eight thousand years ago. Until recently the Innu were known as the Montagnais and Naskapi people, but now they prefer to be called by the name they have for themselves. There are about thirty thousand Innu; most live in nine communities in Quebec. About three thousand Innu live in the Labrador communities of Sheshatshiu and Natuashish.

Before the 1960s when they were settled in villages, the Labrador Innu were nomadic, spending most of the year in nutshimit, the interior of their lands, traveling in small family groups, following the caribou, and living in tents. The men hunted, trapped, and fished. Women tended the children, gathering and preparing food, making tools and clothing. Children also helped out—doing chores, learning from their elders. Everyone looked out for each other, and sharing was

highly valued. Elders today recount how they were born in a tent in nutshimit. Natuashish elder Joachim Nui recalls how his family snowshoed across the whole of Nitassinan, from James Bay to Sheshatshiu, and to Sept-Îles.

Even after they began living in villages, the Innu continued to spend months in nutshimit during the spring and fall. Nutshimit was the place where they could practise their own way of life and ensure their children learned their language and culture. This was their home, the place where they were happy and healthy. But in the 1980s when NATO fighter jets began flying over their camps, life in nutshimit became unbearable.

NATO, the North Atlantic Treaty Organization, was formed in 1949 after World War II. NATO members are countries in Europe and North America who made a promise to help defend each other if any of them was attacked in a war. In the 1980s Canada invited NATO countries to come to Quebec-Labrador to train their pilots to fly jets at supersonic speeds and treetop levels to evade enemy radar and drop bombs. Opposition to the flight-training was growing in European NATO countries; people were calling for a ban because the flights were too loud and dangerous. Claiming Quebec-Labrador was uninhabited, Canada set up two low-level flight training zones over Nitassinan, as well as a bombing range to drop dummy bombs.

The Innu wrote letters to Canada to protest that the NATO jets were flying over unceded Innu land. Innu leaders held meetings with government sharing stories of how the flights over their camps were an assault, especially for elders and children. They also worried about the impacts of the flights on animals. Their concerns fell on deaf ears.

In 1986 Canada decided to try to convince NATO to set up a Tactical Fighter Centre in Goose Bay. This would mean an increase in the number of flights from almost six thousand and eight hundred to forty thousand, as well as two supersonic training zones and nine bombing ranges, three of them to test live bombs.

This move was the last straw for the Innu. For decades they had seen large tracts of their land seized for hydro, forestry, and mining developments. All these things happened without any consultation with the Innu. They knew they needed to take action; they decided they had to stop the jets.

The Innu began to organize protests. Innu elders, along with men, women, and children walked onto Goose Bay airport runways to stop the NATO jets from taking off. These protests were acts of civil disobedience, a peaceful form of protest that involves breaking the law—in this case, trespassing on military property. Both men and women were arrested for these actions; some of them spent time in jail, sometimes months.

While these protests were happening, the Innu also launched a public information campaign. They found allies among other Indigenous Nations and organizations, as well as from peace groups, churches, unions, women's groups, artists, schools, youth groups, health, social justice, and human rights organizations, as well as politicians across North America and Europe. The Innu also traveled to Geneva to lobby the United Nations Human Rights Commission. The world began to take notice and Canada was forced to pay attention.

When they went to court for their actions, the Innu argued to the judge that the military base runways were on Innu territory, that title to the land lived in their hearts. They argued that their elders' stories were proof that the land belonged to the Innu. They had never signed a treaty surrendering their land to Canada, therefore they had not broken any laws, but simply walked on their own land. Judge James Igloliorte agreed with them, ruling the people standing trial had reasonable grounds to believe that the land belonged to them. He stated: "Through their knowledge of ancestry and kinship, they have shown that none of their people ever gave away rights to the land to Canada, and this is an honest belief each person holds." He went on to say that it was not reasonable to assume that the Crown had "magically" acquired title to the land.

This ruling was quickly overturned in a higher court. However, after these protests, both governments and industry understood that the Innu had to be consulted when any developments were being proposed on their lands. To this day, the Innu continue to fight for their rights.

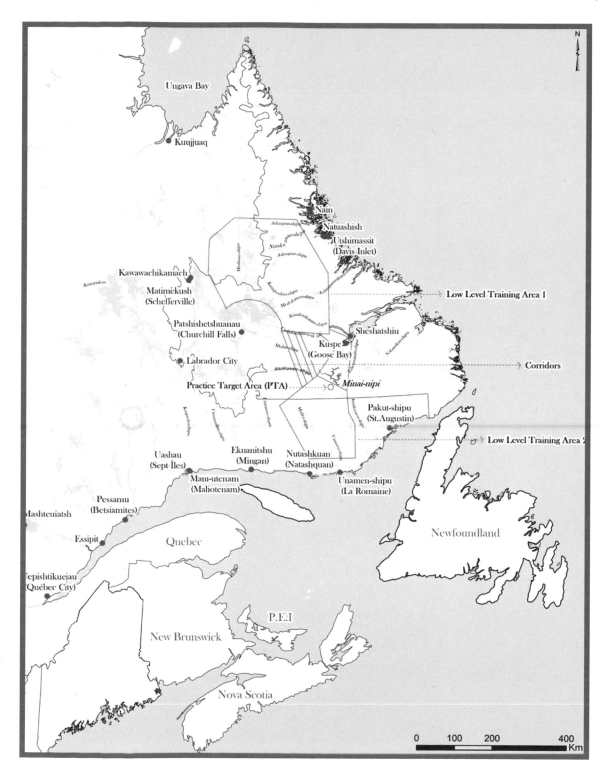

Ungava Bay

Kuujjuaq

Nain
Natuashish
Ashuapun-shipu
Utshen-shipu
Utshimassit
(Davis Inlet)
Nutaku
Ashuapun-shipu

Kawawachikamach
Kauapskau
Matimekush
(Schefferville)
Kanapis-shiuashipu
Low Level Training Area 1
Meshu-shipu
Ashkimashana-shipu
Meshkanau-shipu
Patshishetshuanau
(Churchill Falls)
Kanukal-unnu-shipu
Sheshatshiu
Nekashan-shipu
Kuspe
(Goose Bay)
Labrador City
Mishaushipu
Corridors
Atuakameu-shipu
Practice Target Area (PTA)
Minai-nipi
Mishta-shipu
Pakut-shipu
(St. Augustin)
Kamshasu-shipu
Middle-shipu
Uashau-shipu
Low Level Training Area 2
Uashau
(Sept Îles)
Ekuanitshu
(Mingan)
Nutashkuan
(Natashquan)
Mani-utenam
(Maliotenam)
Unamen-shipu
(La Romaine)
Pessamu
(Betsiamites)
Mashteuiatsh
Essipit
Quebec
Newfoundland
Uepishtikueiau
(Québec City)

P.E.I

New Brunswick

Nova Scotia

N

0   100   200   400
Km

Aimuna

A

a P question marker

aiamieu VTA s/he says to someone; syn *aimieu*

aianimuanitsh *See* **aianimuanu**

aianimuanu VII, IMPERS there is a conversation, discussion going on; syn *aiminanu*

aianimueu VTA s/he talks, speaks to someone; syn *aimieu*

aiashikueu VAI, REDUP s/he shouts, cries out

aiashtunepanu VAI, REDUP s/he mutters

aiasseu VAI s/he puts down a flooring of fir branches; syn *anasseu*

aiatshipaniu VAI, REDUP s/he moves in place, swings

aieshkushiteu VAI s/he has tired legs

aieshkushteteu VAI s/he has tired legs, feet; syn *aieshkukateu*

aimu VAI s/he, it (anim) talks

akau P, LOC behind, hidden from view

akua P watch out! be careful!

akua tuta LOCU be careful *See* **akua, tutam^u**

akuan take it from the water *See* **akuaneu**

akuaneu VTA s/he removes it (anim) from the water

akuashitatshimeu VTA s/he drags him/her, it (anim) from the water

akunahk they press something against something *See* **akunam^u**

akunam^u VTI s/he holds, presses something against another object

akunishkueun NI cap, hat

ama P, NEG not; syn *apu*

ama tapuetakanu LOCU it is forbidden; it is not allowed, acceptable

amiu VAI s/he gets down (from where s/he climbed up)

amiuatsh they get down *See* **amiu**

an P that one

anasseian *See* **anasseu**

anasseu VAI s/he puts down a flooring of fir branches in it

anita P, LOC there (close)

anite P, LOC there

anitshenat they/them *See* **an**

apashui NI long pole used in different types of dwellings

apashuia *See* **apashui**

apatshitat *See* **apatshitau**

apatshitau VAI+O s/he uses something; syn *apashtau*

apu P, NEG not

apu VAI s/he sits

apu tapuetakanit LOCU it is forbidden; it is not allowed, acceptable

apu … ut P, NEG not (past tense)

ashameu VTA s/he gives food to someone

ashamikauian I am given something to eat *See* **ashameu**

ashikuateu VTA s/he yells out to, at someone

ashikueu VAI s/he yells, it (anim) calls out

ashini/ashinin NI stone, rock

ashinina *See* **ashini**

ashinit on a rock *See* **ashini**

ashit NA bough

ashitatsh *See* **ashit**

ashititsh *See* **ashit**

ashpikuatakanu *See* **ashpikuateu**

ashpikuateu VII it is embroidered

ashu-mineu VTA s/he gives him/her something s/he received

ashu-minitak^u *See* **ashu-mineu**

assi/assin NI moss, land, earth, ground

assikumaniapi NI metal wire, cable

assikumaniapia *See* **assikumaniapi**

assit/assitsh *See* **assi**

atamishkuau *See* **atamishkueu**

atamishkueu VTA s/he gives thanks

atatsheikan/atatshenikan NI fence
atatsheikanit/atatshenikanitsh
  See atatsheikan/atatshenikan
ati- PREV begin to, while
atikᵘ NA caribou
atikua See atikᵘ
au P, DEM this
auass NA child
auassat/auassatsh children See auass
auen PRO who; someone
aueshish NA animal
aueshishat/aueshishatsh See aueshish

E
e PREV when, that (+conj)
e niuashit See e, niuashu
ehe P yes; syn *eshe*
eka P, NEG not, don't
eka See eshkᵘ eka
eku P and then
ekue P then; also; syn *kuet*
ekuta P, LOC it is at this (close) place that
ekute P, LOC it is at this place that
Enik NA Eric
eshimakuak See ishimakuan
eshimakuatsh See ishimakuan
eshinakushit See ishinakushu
eshkᵘ P still, again, more
eshkᵘ eka LOCU before
eshkuapekak See ishkuapekan
eshkuapekatsh See ishkuapekan
etatu P more
eti-pitsheian while I enter… See ati-, pitsheu
eti-pitsheiatsh as we go inside… See ati-, pitsheu
eti-utakussitsh while it was evening…
  See ati-, utakussu
etueuekutsh See itueueku

I
iakua See akua
iamiuat they get down See amiu
iapitsh P even so, also, as well; syn *iapit*

iat P even so, also, as well; syn *iapit; ait*
inanu VII, IMPERS it is said, people say
inniminan NI blueberry
inniminana See inniminan
innishu VAI s/he is intelligent
innu NA person, Innu, human being
innu-assi/innu-assin NI Innu territory
innuat/innuatsh See innu
innu-pakueshikan NA bannock
innutshuap NI tent
innutshuapa See innutshuap
innutshuapit/innutshuapitsh in the tent
  See innutshuap
innu-uepashtashun NI Innu flag
innu-ut NI canoe; syn *innu-ush*
innu-utit in a canoe See innu-ut
innu-utshimau NA chief
innu-utshimaua See innu-utshimau
innu-utshimauatsh Innu leaders See innu-utshimau
ishi- PREV in a certain way
ishi-anasseuk I put down a floor of boughs in a certain
  way See ishi-, anasseu
ishi-kusseiakatamuk I bait something in a certain way
  See ishi-, kusseiakatamᵘ
ishimakuan VII it has a certain smell
ishinakuan VII it has a certain look
ishinakuan VII it is necessary that
ishinakuannit See ishinakuan
ishinakuannu See ishinakuan
ishinakushu VAI s/he has to…
ishinikashun NI name
ishitatshimeu VTA s/he drives someone somewhere
ishi-uepinikusseuk See ishi-, uepinikusseu
ishkanitipishkaua P all night
ishkuapekan VII it (stringlike) is a certain length
ishkueu NA woman
ishkueuat women See ishkueu
ishkutet See ishkuteu
ishkuteu NI fire
ishpitenimeu VTA s/he has esteem, respect, high regard
  for someone
issishueu VAI s/he says

iteu VTA s/he says something to someone

itikauiat we were told *See* **iteu**

itinanapan *See* **itu**

itinatsh we (excl.) do something *See* **itu**

itu VAI s/he is thus; this happens to her/him; s/he does something

itueueku VAI it (anim) makes a certain noise when flowing

ituteht they go somewhere on foot *See* **ituteu**

ituteu VAI s/he goes somewhere on foot

K

ka PREV past

ka PREV the one(s) who, the thing(s) that

ka PREV will

ka ishinakuannit the one that has a certain look *See* **ka, ishinakuan**

ka makunakaniht/ka makunakanitsh the ones who are arrested *See* **ka, makunakanu**

ka nipaik the one that I killed *See* **ka, nipaieu**

ka papamishkat s/he travelled by water *See* **ka, papamishkau**

ka papamishkatsh they travelled by water *See* **ka, papamishkau**

ka taian I was there *See* **ka, tau**

ka tshikamuniti/ka tshikamunitshi the ones (obv) that are attached *See* **ka, tshikamu**

ka tshinapishkat the things that are pointed, sharp *See* **ka, tshinapishkau**

ka tueunitshi *See* **ka, tueu**

ka tueutshi *See* **ka, tueu**

ka uasheshkuianitsh/ka uasheshkunanit the one that is blue *See* **ka, uasheshkuiau**

ka uitshinatsh we camped somewhere *See* **ka, uitshu**

kakashiminisht-nishekuiapin NI razor wire

kakashiminisht-nishekuapinnu *See* **kakashiminisht-nishekuiapin**

kakussesht NAP fisherman

kamakunueshiht/kamakunueshitsh *See* **kamakunuesht**

kamakunueshiutapaia *See* **kamakunueshiutapan**

kamakunueshiutapan NI police car

kamakunueshiutapana *See* **kamakunueshiutapan**

kamakunueshiutapanit/kamakunueshiutapanitsh *See* **kamakunueshiutapan**

kamakunuesht NAP police officer

Kanata TOP Canada

kanataut/kanatuiut NAP hunter

ka-nitanaua *See* **tau**

ka-nitikua *See* **iteu**

ka-nititikua it says to me *See* **iteu**

kapakapaniss NIP bomb

kapakapanissa *See* **kapakapaniss**

kapakapanit NIP dynamite, explosives

kapakapanitshi *See* **kapakapanit**

kapiminashinitshi *See* **kapiminasht**

kapiminashitsh *See* **kapiminasht**

kapiminasht NAP airplane; syn *kapimipanit, kapiminat*

kapimipanitasht NAP driver

kapita P, INTERJ wait; syn *eka pitama*

kassinu P each one, each, all; syn *mishue*

katakᵘ P, LOC far; syn *uiau*

ka-titipapitshepanua *See* **titipapitshepanu**

katshi PREV past

katshi aianimuanitsh after they had a discussion *See* **katshi, aianimuanu**

katshi ashu-minitakᵘ after s/he gave us something *See* **katshi, ashu mineu**

katshi manukashuiat/katshi manukashunatsh after we set up our tent *See* **katshi, manukashu**

katshi nashkumuian/katshi nashkumunan after I gave thanks *See* **katshi, nashkumu**

katshi takushipatain after you arrived driving *See* **katshi, takushipatau**

katshi tshetshishepaushinit after it was morning *See* **katshi, tshetshishepaushu**

katshi tshishi-utshimau-aiminanut after the meeting was finished *See* **katshi, tshishi-, utshimau-aiminanu**

katshishapissiteshinit *See* **katshishapissitesht**

katshishapissiteshinitsh *See* **katshishapissitesht**

katshishapissitesht NIP stove

katshishipanishiht *See* **katshishipanisht**

katshishipanishitsh *See* **katshishipanisht**

katshishipanisht NAP jet

katshitinau *See* **katshitineu**

katshitineu VTA s/he catches something (anim)

ka-tshititaiaiaua *See* **tau**

ka-tshititananua *See* **tau**

kie P and, also, too

kuashkuashkuepaniu VAI/REDUP s/he jumps up and down

kuashkuepaniu VAI s/he jumps, throws him/herself into something

kueshtetshe P, LOC on the other side (at a certain distance)

kuessiman/kuessipan P it's my turn

kuet P then; syn *ekue*

kuetshimeu VTA s/he asks someone something

kuetuetsh *See* **kutueu**

kuishkᵘ P straight; directly

kuneu VTA s/he knocks, takes something down

kushkan NI fish hook

kushkaniapi NI fishing line; fishing gear

kushkannu *See* **kushkan**

kushkap NI fishing spot

kushkapitsh to his fishing spot *See* **kushkap**

kushkun P straight; directly; syn *kuishkᵘ*

kushkunnu *See* **kushkun**

kushtatshiht they are afraid *See* **kushtatshu**

kushtatshimeu VTA s/he frightens him/her by sound

kushtatshimikutshenat they must be frightened by something (anim) *See* **kushtatshimeu**

kushtatshimikutshenitshi they must be frightened by something (anim) *See* **kushtatshimeu**

kushtatshu VAI s/he, it (anim) is afraid

kushtatshuatsh *See* **kushtatshu**

kushtikuan VII it is dangerous

kushtineu VTA s/he prevents someone, something (anim)

kusseiakataman *See* **kusseiakatamᵘ**

kusseiakatamᵘ VTI s/he baits something

kusset *See* **kusseu**

kusseu VAI s/he is fishing

kusseu-apatshitaun NI fishing gear

kutaueu VTA s/he knocks him/her down

kutaukauiat we were knocked to the ground *See* **kutaueu**

kutuan NI outdoor hearth, fireplace

kutuanit around the fireplace *See* **kutuan**

kutueu VAI s/he makes a fire

kutunnuepipuneshu VAI s/he is ten years old

M

ma P is it not the case that…?

maiashiteu VAI s/he gathers fir branches; syn *manashteu*

mak P and

mak iat LOCU and even; syn *mak iapit*

makunakaniht *See* **makunakanu**

makunakanitsh *See* **makunakanu**

makunakanu VAI, PASS s/he is arrested, in prison

makunakanuat they are arrested *See* **makunakanu**

makunamᵘ VTI s/he holds something tight

makuneu VTA s/he arrests someone

makunititshepitakaniht they are handcuffed *See* **makunititshepitakanu**

makunititshepitakanu VAI, PASS s/he is handcuffed

makunitsheuiu VAI s/he clenches her/his hand, makes a fist

makupitakanitsh they are tied up *See* **makupitakanu**

makupitakanu VAI, PASS s/he is tied up

mamuituat/mamuituatsh VAI, PL, RECIP they have a gathering, they gather with each other

mamuituht *See* **mamuituat**

manashteu VAI s/he gathers fir

Manimat NA Manimat, Mary Martha

manipiteu VTA s/he pulls something (anim) off

manipiteuat/manipiteuatsh they pull something off *See* **manipiteu**

manitatshimeu VTA s/he drags, hauls someone away, removes someone

manukashu VAI s/he sets up a tent

manukashuat *See* **manukashu**

manukashuiat/manukashunatsh *See* **manukashu**

mashikamᵘ VTI s/he fights something

mashikenan we fight something *See* **mashikamᵘ**

mashkᵘ NA bear

mashkua *See* **mashkᵘ**

matinenitamᵘ VTI s/he is smart about something

matshi P go ahead! go away!

mau VAI s/he cries

mauatsh P, INTERJ no; syn *mauat*

maushu VAI s/he picks berries

metikat P slowly, gently

miakunaht they arrest someone *See* **makuneu**

mianitak[u] s/he gives something (anim) to us
  See **mineu**

Minai-nipi TOP Minai-nipi

Minai-nipit/Minai-nipitsh *See* **Minai-nipi**

minakunatsh they arrest someone *See* **makuneu**

minameu VTA s/he, it (anim) smells something (anim)

minashkuat/minashkuatsh P, LOC in the bush,
  in the woods

mineu VTA s/he gives something to someone

minuat/minuatsh P again, once more

minuat *See* **minuau**

minuau VII it is good, right

minuenitak *See* **minuenitam**[u]

minuenitam[u] VTI s/he is pleased, happy, satisfied

mishapishkau VII it (mineral) is big

mishimameu VTA s/he, it (anim) smells something
  (anim); syn *ishimameu, minameu*

mishimenitamishkaku *See* **mishimenitam**[u]

mishimenitam[u] VTI s/he worries about something

mishishtu/mishitu VAI it (anim) is big

mishta- PREV big, very, a lot

mishta-aiashikueuatsh they cry out in anger
  See **mishta-, aiashikueu**

mishta-aiatshipaniu it (anim) swings wildly
  See **mishta-, aiatshipaniu**

mishta-innishuat they are very smart
  See **mishta-, innishu**

mishta-makunitsheuiu s/he clenches her/his fists
  tightly *See* **mishta-, makunitsheuiu**

mishta-matinenitamuatsh they are very smart
  See **mishta-, matinenitam**[u]

mishta-mishishtu/mishta-mishitu s/he, it (anim)
  is very big *See* **mishta-, mishishtu/mishitu**

mishta-muau *See* **mishta-, mueu**

mishta-nutin it is very windy *See* **mishta-, nutin**

mishta-nutishu it is very windy *See* **mishta-, nutishu**

mishta-shutshishiu s/he is very strong
  See **mishta-, shutshishiu**

mishta-tshisheuepanu something makes a deafening
  boom passing by *See* **mishta-, tshisheuepanu**

mishta-tshishuaiku s/he is made very angry
  by something *See* **mishta-, tshishuaiku**

mishta-tshishuapuat/mishta-tshishuapuatsh they are
  very angry *See* **mishta-, tshishuapu**

mishta-uitshitu it tastes delicious *See* **mishta-, uitshitu**

mishtik[u] NA tree

mishtikua *See* **mishtik**[u]

mishtikut/mishtikutsh *See* **mishtik**[u]

mishue P each one, each, all; syn *kassinu*

Missinak[u] NA Master of water animals
  (character in stories)

mitsheia VII there are many; syn *mitshena*

mitshetuau P many times

mitshimin hold on *See* **mitshimineu**

mitshimineu VTA s/he holds something in place using
  an object, clamps something

muanan/muauiai *See* **mueu**

mueu VTA s/he eats something (anim)

mukaun *See* **mueu**

muk[u] P but, only

mumesheiai/mumeshenan *See* **mumesheu**

mumesheu VTI s/he eats fish

mushinau P always

mushu VAI s/he picks berries; syn *maushu*

mutatam[u] VTI it (anim) catches in its mouth
  something moving; syn *nutatam*[u]

N

naiamishkuenu VAI s/he nods; syn *nanamishkuenu*

naikam[u] VTI s/he cleans something

naikamuk I clean something *See* **naikam**[u]

nakapaniu VAI s/he falls down, ducks down to hide

nakatuapameu VTA s/he watches, keeps an eye
  on someone, something (anim)

nakatuenimeu VTA s/he watches over someone,
  looks after someone, keeps someone safe

nakatuenimiku *See* **nakatuenimeu**

nakatuenitam[u] VTI s/he watches, pays attention to something

nakatuenitenan *See* **nakatuenitam**[u]

namaieu PRO it is not someone, something

namesh NA fish

namesha *See* **namesh**

nanamishkuenu VAI, REDUP s/he nods her/his head up and down

Nanass NA Nanass

nanatuapatam[u] VTI s/he looks for something

nanatu-tshissenitam[u] VTI, REDUP s/he tries to find something out

nanatu-tshissenitamuatsh they try to find something out *See* **nanatu-tshissenitam**[u]

nanitam P always

napeu NA man

napeuat/napeuatsh *See* **napeu**

nashaueu VTA s/he, it (anim) follows someone on foot; syn *nashueu*

nashinakanu VTA, PASS s/he is lowered by hand

nashkuepitam[u] VTI s/he takes something quickly in passing

nashkumau *See* **nashkumeu**

nashkumeu VTA s/he thanks someone

nashkumu VAI s/he gives thanks

nashkumuian/nashkumunan *See* **nashkumu**

nasht P quite, completely, very; syn *nashtesh*

nataht they go to meet someone *See* **nateu**

natatsh they go to meet them *See* **nateu**

nateu VTA s/he goes to meet up with someone

natime go meet someone *See* **nateu**

natshi-kusseini if you go fishing *See* **natshi-kusseu**

natshi-kussen *See* **natshi-kusseu**

natshi-kusseu VAI s/he goes fishing with a line

natshinakanu VAI, PASS s/he, it (anim) is pushed away by hand

natshipanu VII it stops moving

natshipanua *See* **natshipanu**

natshi-uapatam[u] VTI s/he goes to see something

natuapame go see her/him *See* **natuapameu**

natuapameu VTA s/he goes to see or get someone or something (anim)

natuapataman I fetch something *See* **natuapatam**[u]

natuapatam[u] VTI s/he goes to see or fetch something

natutam[u] VTI s/he listens to something

natutatak[u] *See* **natutueu**

natutueu VTA s/he listens to someone, something (anim)

naunashu VAI s/he packs her/his bags

naunashunai/naunashunan *See* **naunashu**

ne PRO, DEM that one

nekaniss NI tin can

nekanissit around a can *See* **nekaniss**

nenu *See* **ne**

nepaian *See* **nipau**

nepak *See* **nipaieu**

ni-, nit-, n- PFX I, me, my, we, us, our

nika I/we will *See* **ni-, ka**

nika mother, mom *See* **ni-, ukauia/ukauna**

nika muanan/nika muauiai we will eat *See* **nika, mueu**

nika mumesheiai/nika mumeshenan we will eat fish *See* **nika, mumesheu**

nika naunashunai we will pack up *See* **nika, naunashu**

nika pimuteiai/nika pimutenan we will walk *See* **nika, pimuteu**

nika tshimatai I will set it up *See* **nika, tshimatau**

nika ui katshitinau I want to catch something (anim) *See* **nika, ui, katshitineu**

nikan P ahead, in front; in the future

nikanishinanat our relatives *See* **ni-, uikanisha**

nikaui/nikaun my mother *See* **ni-, ukauia/ukauna**

nikuashkuashkuepaniun I jump up and down *See* **ni-, kuashkuashkuepaniu**

nikuashkuepaniun I jump suddenly *See* **ni-, kuashkuepaniu**

nikuetshimau I ask someone something *See* **ni-, kuetshimeu**

nikuneiai/nikunenan we take something down by hand *See* **ni-, kuneu**

nikushkan my fish hook *See* **ni-, kushkan**

nikushkaniapi my fishing line *See* **ni-, kushkaniapi**

nikushtatshin I am afraid *See* **ni-, kushtatshu**

nikushtinaiatsh/nikushtinananat we prevent them *See* **ni-, kushtineu**

nikusseu-apatshitauna my fishing gear *See* **ni-, kusseun apatshitaun**

nimai I cry *See* **ni-, mau**

nimakunamuai I hold something tight *See* **ni-, makunam**ᵘ

nimamuinai we gather *See* **ni-, mamuituatsh**

niman I cry *See* **ni-, mau**

nimanitatshimikunaiatsh we are taken away *See* **ni-, manitatshimeu**

nimashkuaitsheu VAI s/he holds a protest

nimaushutan we picked berries *See* **ni-, maushu**

niminamau I smell her/him *See* **ni-, minameu**

niminuenitei/niminueniten I am happy *See* **ni-, minuenitam**ᵘ

nimishimamau I smell someone *See* **ni-, mishimameu**

nimishta-aiashikuei I shout, cry out *See* **ni-, mishta , aiashikueu**

nimishta-muau I eat a lot *See* **ni-, mishta-, mueu**

nimushunaiapan we picked berries *See* **ni-, mushu**

nin PRO I, me

nikapaniuiatsh *See* **nakapaniu**

ninakatuapamaiaiatsh *See* **ni-, nakatuapameu**

ninakatuapamauatsh I watch them *See* **ni-, nakatuapameu**

ninakatuenimikuatsh/ninakatuenimikuht they watch over me *See* **ni-, nakatuenimeu**

ninameshim my fish *See* **ni-, namesh**

ninan PRO we, us (me and her/him/them)

ninanatuapaten I look for something *See* **ni-, nanatuapatam**ᵘ

ninashakuat they follow me on foot *See* **ni-, nashaueu**

ninashauau I follow her/him *See* **ni-, nashaueu**

ninatshi-uapatenan we go to see something *See* **ni-, natshi-uapatam**ᵘ

ninimashkuaitshenan we hold a protest *See* **ni-, nimashkuaitsheu**

ninutshikashunai we deal with *See* **ni-, nutshikashu**

nipa PREV I/we would

nipa tshi a petutei can I come? *See* **nipa, tshi, a, petuteu**

nipa ui nipaiau I would like to kill it *See* **nipa, ui, nipaieu**

nipaiau *See* **nipaieu**

nipaieu VTA s/he kills someone, something (anim)

nipaik *See* **nipaieu**

nipakuaten I am eager, impatient *See* **ni-, pakuateu**

nipashituepaniunan they get themselves over something *See* **pashituepaniu**

nipau VAI s/he sleeps, is asleep

nipetei/nipeten I hear something *See* **ni-, petam**ᵘ

nipi NI water

nipimuteiai/nipimutenan we walk *See* **ni-, pimuteu**

nipishtepatai I run inside *See* **ni-, pishtepatau**

nipitsheiai we go inside *See* **ni-, pitsheu**

nipitshepimipatashin I bounce along *See* **ni-, pitshepimipatashu**

nipuamun I dream *See* **ni-, puamu**

nipuamutamuan I dream about something *See* **ni-, puamutam**ᵘ

nipuatamuai *See* **ni-, puatam**ᵘ

nipuatei I dream *See* **ni-, puatam**ᵘ

nipushikunanat they loaded us on board *See* **ni-, pushieu**

nishakatshueiai we get to the top *See* **ni-, shakatshueu**

nishaputuetenan we walk past *See* **ni-, shaputueteu**

nishatshinissetaiau I take her/him by the hand *See* **ni-, shatshinissetaieu**

nisheku-unakan NI tin can; syn *nekaniss*

nisheku-unakanitsh *See* **nisheku-unakan**

nishetshishin I am frightened *See* **ni-, shetshishu**

nishi- PREV in a certain way; syn *ishi-*

nishi-aiasseian I put down a flooring of fir branches in a certain way *See* **nishi-, aiasseu**

nishk NA goose

nishka *See* **nishk**

nishkassikanit/nishkassikanitsh against my chest *See* **ni-, ushkassikan**

nishkueu NA woman; syn *ishkueu*

nishkueuatsh women *See* **nishkueu**

nishtam P first

nishupishimua P for two months

nissishueu VAI s/he, it (anim) says; syn *issishueu*

nitaianimuaiaiatsh we talk to them
   See **ni-**, **aianimueu**

nitaianimuei I say to him/her See **ni-**, **aianimueu**

nitaieshkushiten I have tired feet
   See **ni-**, **aieshkushiteu**

nitaieshkushtetei I have tired legs, feet
   See **ni-**, **aieshkushiteu**

nitaiminan we talk See **aimu**

nitakuananan we reel it in See **ni-**, **akuaneu**

nitakuashitatshimaiai we reel it in
   See **ni-**, **akuashitatshimeu**

nitakunamuai/nitakunamuan I hold something
   in my hands See **ni-**, **takunam**ᵘ

nitakushinai we arrive See **ni-**, **takushinu**

nitapinan we sit See **ni-**, **apu**

nitapishikuashkuau I pass a stick through it (anim)
   See **ni-**, **tapishikuashkueu**

nitapishikuashkutshimau I hang it (anim) on a stick
   See **ni-**, **tapishikuashkutshimeu nitapuetuau** I follow
his/her order See **ni-**, **tapuetueu**

nitashikuatikunai s/he yells at us See **ni-**, **ashikuateu**

nitashikuei/nitashikuen I yell out See **ni-**, **ashikueu**

nitassinan our land See **ni-**, **assi/assin**

nitassinat See **ni-**, **assi**

nitassinatsh See **ni-**, **assi**

nitati-uitsheuau as I go with her/him...
   See **ni-**, **ati-**, **uitsheueu**

nitau- PREV good, well

nitau-kusset s/he is good at fishing See **nitau-**, **kusseu**

nitei/niten my heart See **ni-**, **utei/uten**

nitetapinai we sit on a seat See **ni-**, **tetapu**

niteu VTA s/he says something to someone; syn *iteu*

nitikunaiatsh they say to us See **ni-**, **niteu**

nitipatshimushtakᵘ s/he recounts a story to me
   See **ni-**, **tipatshimushtueu**

nitipatshimushtakunai s/he recounts stories to us
   See **ni-**, **tipatshimushtueu**

nitishitatshimikunan they drive us somewhere
   See **ni-**, **ishitatshimeu**

nitishi-tepuatikunanat they shout at us in a certain
way See **ni-**, **ishi**, **tepuateu**

nitishpitenimikuat/nitishpitenimikuatsh they are
   proud of me See **ni-**, **ishpitenimeu**

nitissishuen I say See **ni-**, **issishueu**

nititanan we are here See **ni-**, **tau**

nititau I say to someone See **ni-**, **iteu**

nititikᵘ s/he says to me See **ni-**, **iteu**

nitshimushapinan we spy, watch secretly
   See **ni-**, **tshimushapu**

nitshinaia/nitshinana our tent See **ni-**, **uitsh**

nitshinat/nitshinatsh See **ni-**, **uitsh**

nitshinnuatsh my people See **ni-**, **uitshinnua**

nitshipishkuananat we block their passage
   See **ni-**, **tshipishkueu**

nitshishuapin I'm angry See **ni-**, **tshishuapu**

nitshissenimau I know something
   See **ni-**, **tshissenimeu**

nitshitapamau I watch her/him See **ni-**, **tshitapameu**

nitshitapamauat I watch them See **ni-**, **tshitapameu**

nitshitinamuai/nitshitinamuan I fetch something
   quickly See **ni-**, **tshitinam**ᵘ

nitshitinikunanat they fetch us quickly
   See **ni-**, **tshitineu**

nitshiuetaikuat/nitshiuetanikuatsh they take me home
   See **ni-**, **tshiuetaieu**

nitshiuetatshimikunai s/he drives us back
   See **ni-**, **tshiuetatshimeu**

nituss my aunt See **ni-**, **utussa**

nitussat/nitussatsh my aunts See **ni-**, **utussa**

niuashit See **niuashu**

niuashu VII, DIM the water is shallow

nuapatinikᵘ See **ni-**, **uapatinieu**

nueuetatshimunai we crawl outside
   See **ni-**, **ueuetatshimu**

nueutshipitikᵘ s/he holds me tightly in her/his arms
   See **ni-**, **ueutshipiteu**

nui I, we want (to) See **ni-**, **ui**

nui uitamuautsh I want to tell them something
   See **ni-**, **ui**, **uitamueu**

nuitsheuakaiatsh our friends See **ni-**, **uitsheuakaia**

nuitsheuakananat our friends *See* **ni-, uitsheuakana**

nuitsheuakanat our friends *See* **ni-, uitsheuakana**

nuitshipatamikuatsh they leave running with me
See **ni-, uitshipatameu**

nukum my grandmother, grandma *See* **ni-, ukuma**

nukumish my uncle *See* **ni-, ukumisha**

nunuitatshimunan we crawl outside
See **ni-, unuitatshimu**

nuta NA, VOC dad, daddy

nutatamᵘ VTI it (anim) catches in its mouth
something moving

nutaui/nutaun my father *See* **ni-, utauia/utauna**

nutim P all, whole

nutin VII it is windy

nutishu VII, DIM it is windy

nutshikashu VAI s/he deals with

nutshimit/nutshimitsh P, LOC in the bush, in the country

P

pakashtuepaniu VAI s/he, it (anim) plunges
into the water

pakashtuepaniun *See* **pakashtuepaniu**

pakuateu VAI s/he is eager, impatient with regard
to someone

pakueshikai NA bread, bannock; syn *pakueshikan*

papaituat VAI, PL they arrive together running or driving

papamishkat *See* **papamishkau**

papamishkatsh *See* **papamishkau**

papamishkau VAI, REDUP s/he, it (anim) travels around
on or in the water

papashtakᵘ NA board; syn *papatshitak*ᵘ

papashtakua *See* **papashtak**ᵘ

papashtakut *See* **papashtak**ᵘ

papatshitakᵘ NA board

papatshitakua *See* **papatshitak**ᵘ

papatshitakutsh *See* **papatshitak**ᵘ

papikuenu VAI s/he smiles

papinanu VII, IMPERS people laugh

papit *See* **papu**

papu VAI s/he laughs

papuashtataian I let it flap in the wind so the dirt
comes off *See* **papuashtatau**

papuashtatau VAI s/he lets something flap in the wind
(to get rid of what sticks to it)

pashituepaniu VAI s/he gets her/himself over,
past something

patashtaimᵘ VTI s/he keeps something flat using
a weight

patashtaimuatsh *See* **patashtaim**ᵘ

patshitat *See* **patshitau**

patshitau VAI s/he lets something fall, drop;
syn *patshititau*

patshitinahk *See* **patshitinam**ᵘ

patshitinamᵘ VTI s/he lets something drop

patshitinatsh *See* **patshitinam**ᵘ

patshititat *See* **patshitititau**

patshitititau VAI s/he lets something fall

patshuianitshuap NI canvas tent

patshuianitshuapit/patshuianitshuapitsh to,
in the tent *See* **patshuianitshuap**

patush P later, after

peikunnu P, NUM ten

peikutshishikua P for one day

peminuanitsh *See* **piminueu**

peminuenanuti *See* **piminuenanu**

pemuteiat *See* **pimuteu**

pemuteiatsh we walk *See* **pimuteu**

peshueu VTI s/he brings someone, something
(anim) here

peshut bring them (anim) *See* **peshueu**

petamᵘ VTI s/he hears something

petueuepanu VAI/VII it comes in this direction
making noise

petueuepanitshi *See* **petueuepanu**

petueuepatamakaia they approach noisily
See **petueuepatamakan**

petueuepatamakan VII it approcahes noisily, running
or driving

petueuepatau VAI s/he, it (anim) approaches noisily,
running or driving

petutei *See* **petuteu**

petuteu VAI s/he or it (anim) comes in this direction
on foot

piatutsheian I go inside *See* **pitutsheu**

pikush NA black fly
pikushatsh black flies *See* **pikush**
pimapekashteu VAI s/he places something stringlike down twisted
piminuanitsh *See* **piminuanu**
piminuanu VII, IMPERS there is cooking, people are cooking; syn *piminuenanu*
piminuenanut *See* **piminuenanu**
piminuenanu VII, IMPERS people are cooking
piminueu VAI s/he cooks
pimipaniht they fly along *See* **pimipanu**
pimipanu VAI/VII it flies along, it swims around, s/he goes along
pimipanuat they fly *See* **pimipanu**
pimipanuatsh they fly *See* **pimipanu**
pimishkaiakuakue if we were paddling *See* **pimishkau**
pimishkau VTA s/he paddles; it (animal) swims
pimueuepanu VAI/VII it makes noise passing by
pimuteiai *See* **pimuteu**
pimuteiat/pimuteiatsh *See* **pimuteu**
pimutenan *See* **pimuteu**
pimutenanu VII there is a walk; people walk
pimutenanut *See* **pimutenanu**
pimutetsh *See* **pimuteu**
pimuteu VAI s/he walks
pimuteuatsh they walk *See* **pimuteu**
pishtepatau VAI s/he, it (anim) rushes, runs inside; syn *pitutepatau*
pishtishu VAI s/he cuts her/himself by accident
pishtishuat/pishtishuatsh they cut themselves by accident *See* **pishtishu**
pitshepimipatashu VAI, DIM s/he (small) bounces along
pitsheu VAI s/he goes inside, enters; syn *pitutsheu*
pitsheuatsh *See* **pitsheu**
pitukaieu VTA s/he brings something (anim) inside
pitukanatsh *See* **pitukaieu**
pitutepataian I run inside *See* **pitutepatau**
pitutepatau VAI s/he, it (anim) rushes, runs inside
pitutshenanut people enter *See* **pitutsheu**
pitutsheu VAI s/he goes inside, enters
puamu VAI s/he dreams, has a dream
puamutam^u VTI s/he dreams something

puass NI bus
puassa *See* **puass**
puassinu *See* **puass**
puassit/puassitsh *See* **puass**
puatam^u VTI s/he dreams about something
Puna NA Paula
pushiakanu VAI, PASS s/he is taken along on a trip
pushiakanuatsh they are taken on a trip *See* **pushiakanu**
pushieu VTA s/he puts him/her on board
pushikuiat we are put on board *See* **pushieu**
pushineu VTA s/he puts him/her on board; syn *pushieu*
pushinikunatsh we are put on board *See* **pushineu**
pushit s/he gets on board *See* **pushu**
pushu VAI s/he embarks, gets on board

SH
shakatshueu VAI s/he arrives at the summit, the top
shaputueteu VAI s/he walks past the limit
shaputueteuat they walk past, beyond *See* **shaputueteu**
shash P already, now, finally
shassikut/shassikutsh P suddenly, all of a sudden
shateiapassipanu VAI the light off the metal is dazzling
shateiapishtepanu VAI the light flashes and dazzles
shatshimeshkat *See* **shatshimeshkau**
shatshimeshkau VII there are a lot of black flies
shatshinissetaieu VTA s/he takes someone by the hand
shatuapekashtau VAI s/he unfolds something stringlike
shatuapekashtauat/shatuapekashtauatsh they unfold something stringlike *See* **shatuapekashtau**
Sheshatshit/Sheshatshitsh *See* **Sheshatshiu**
Sheshatshiu TOP Sheshatshiu
shetshieu VTA s/he frightens, scares someone
shetshiku they are scaring her *See* **shetshieu**
shetshikuian I am frightened by something *See* **shetshieu**
shetshiniku *See* **shetshieu**
shetshishu VAI s/he is scared, frightened
shimakanish NA soldier
shimakanishat/shimakanishatsh army, military *See* **shimakanish**

shipitsh by the river *See* **shipu**

shipu NI river

shutshishi *See* **shutshishiu**

shutshishiu VAI s/he, it (anim) is physically strong

T

taiakuakue if we were there *See* **tau**

taian *See* **tau**

takuan VII it exists, there is

takuatsh *See* **takuan**

takunamᵘ VTI s/he holds something in her/his hands

takushinitsh *See* **takushinu**

takushinu VAI s/he comes, arrives

takushipatain *See* **takushipatau**

takushipatau VAI s/he arrives running or driving

takusseu VAI s/he takes a step

takusseuat/takusseuatsh they take a step
See **takusseu**

tan P how, how many, how much

tan tshipa itinanapan what would happen
See **tan, tshipa, itu**

tan tshipa tutakaiatsh what would be done
See **tan, tshipa, tutakanu**

tapataushu VAI, DIM it (anim, small) flies low

tapataushuat/tapataushuatsh they (anim, small)
fly low *See* **tapataushu**

tapishikuashkueu VTA s/he passes a stick through
something (anim)

tapishikuashkutshimeu VTA s/he hangs something
(anim) on a stick

tapue P really, it's true

tapuetakanit *See* **apu tapuetakanit**

tapuetakanu *See* **ama tapuetakanu**

tapuetueu VTA s/he agrees with him/her, agrees
to his/her request

tatupipuneshu VAI s/he is so many years old

tatshishinu VAI s/he, it (anim) touches up against
a surface; touches ground

tatshishinuat/tatshishinuatsh they touch the surface
See **tatshishinu**

tau VAI s/he, it (anim) is present, is there

tekuannit *See* **takuan**

tekuannitsh *See* **takuan**

tekushiniat we arrive *See* **takushinu**

tekushinit *See* **takushinu**

tepuatakanu VAI, PASS s/he is called

tepuateu VTA s/he shouts, yells at, to someone

tepuateuat they shout at them *See* **tepuateu**

tepueu VAI s/he shouts, cries out

tepueuatsh they shout *See* **tepueu**

tetapu VAI s/he, it (anim) sits on a seat

tetaut/tetautsh P, LOC in the middle

tipatshimushtueu VTA s/he tells someone a real life
story, recounts an event

tipatutamᵘ VTI s/he tells what s/he has seen

tipatuteu VTA s/he tells something (anim) that
s/he has seen

tipenitamᵘ VTI s/he controls, governs something

titipapitshepanu VII it (stringlike) gets rolled,
wound around an object

titipinatshishtakanu VII, PASS it (line) is wound
around something

tueu VTI s/he, it (anim) lands from the air

tueunan NI airport

tueunanit *See* **tueunan**

tueunitshi *See* **tueu**

tueutshi *See* **tueu**

tuta *See* **tutamᵘ**

tutahk *See* **tutamᵘ**

tutakaiaiatsh *See* **tutakanu**

tutakanu VII, PASS it is done

tutamᵘ VTI s/he does something

TSH

tshash P already, now, finally; syn *shash*

tshe PEV will

tshe apatshitat s/he will use something
See **tshe, apatshitau**

tshe ishi-anasseuk I will put down a flooring
of boughs in a certain way *See* **tshe, ishi-, anasseu**

tshe ishi-kusseiakatamuk I will bait something
in a certain way *See* **tshe, ishi-, kusseiakatamᵘ**

tshe ishi-uepinikusseuk I will cast a fishing line
in a certain way *See* **tshe, ishi-, uepinikusseu**

tshe itinatsh we (excl.) will do something
  See **tshe, itu**
tshe nishi-aiasseian I will put down a flooring of fir
  branches in a certain way *See* **tshe, nishi-, aiasseu**
tshe piminuanitsh there will be cooking going on
  See **tshe, piminuanu**
tshe tutahk they will do something *See* **tshe, tutam**ᵁ
tshekat P almost
tshekuan NI something, thing
tshekuan PRO what, which thing
tshekuannu uet/tshekuannu uitsh LOCU why in the
  world is…?
tshematatsh they put something up *See* **tshimatau**
tsheshka P for nothing
tshetshi PREV so that, in order to
tshetshi aianimuanitsh in order for them to have
  a discussion *See* **tshetshi, aianimuanu**
tshetshi anasseian in order for me to put down a floor
  See **tshetshi, anasseu**
tshetshi eka pimipaniht so that they don't fly
  See **tshetshi, eka, pimipanu**
tshetshi kusseiakataman in order for me to bait
something *See* **tshetshi, kusseiakatam**ᵁ
tshetshi kusset in order for her/him to fish
  See **tshetshi, kusseu**
tshetshi mamuituht in order for them to gather
  together *See* **tshetshi, mamuituat**
tshetshi manukashuiat in order for us to set up a tent
  See **tshetshi, manukashu**
tshetshi nitau-kusset so that s/he can fish well
  See **tshetshi, nitau-, kusseu**
tshetshi patshitinahk/tshetshi patshitinatsh in order
  for them to let something drop
  See **tshetshi, patshitinam**ᵁ
tshetshi piminuenanut in order for people to cook
  See **tshetshi, piminuenanu**
tshetshi pimuteiatsh in order for us to walk
  See **tshetshi, pimuteu**
tshetshi pimutenanut in order for people to walk
  See **tshetshi, pimutenanu**
tshetshi pitutshenanut for people to enter
  See **tshetshi, pitutsheu**

tshetshi tshishitet/tshetshi tshishitetsh so that
  it will be hot *See* **tshetshi, tshishiteu**
tshetshi tshishkutamatishuht/tshetshi
tshishkutamashuatsh so they can practice
  See **tshetshi, tshishkutama(ti)shu**
tshetshi uepinaman so that I can cast
  See **tshetshi, uepinam**ᵁ
tshetshi uitamukau in order for me to tell them
  something *See* **tshetshi, uitamueu**
tshetshi upauht/tshetshi upautsh so that they fly,
  take off *See* **tshetshi, upau**
tshetshishepapan VII it is early in the morning
tshetshishepaushinit *See* **tshetshishepaushu**
tshetshishepaushu VII it is morning
tshi PREV able, can
tshi uitsheutin *See* **tshi, uitsheueu**
tshi-, tshit-, tsh- PFX you, your, we, our
tshiashi- PREV old
tshiashi-utakunishkueun her/his old cap
  See **tshiashi-, u-, akunishkueun**
tshika PREV will, going to
tshika makunakanuat they will be arrested
  See **tshika, makunakanu**
tshika mashikenan we will fight something
  See **tshika, mashikam**ᵁ
tshika mukaun you will be eaten *See* **tshika, mueu**
tshika nakatuenimiku it (anim) will look after him/her
  See **tshika, nakatuenimeu**
tshika nanatu-tshissenitamuatsh they will try to find
  something out, find a way
  See **tshika, nanatu-tshissenitam**ᵁ
tshika naunashunan we will pack our bags
  See **tshika, naunashu**
tshika pakashtuepaniun you throw yourself into
  the water *See* **tshika, pakashtuepaniu**
tshika pimipanuat/tshika pimipanuatsh they will fly
  See **tshika, pimipanu**
tshika pimuteu s/he will walk *See* **tshika, pimuteu**
tshika pushiakanuatsh they would be taken on a trip
  See **tshika, pushiakanu**
tshika tipenitamᵁ s/he will govern, control
  See **tshika, tipenitam**ᵁ

tshika tshi a uitsheutin?/tshika tshi uitsheutin a? can I go with you? *See* **a, tshika, tshi, uitsheueu**

tshika tshishkutamuakanu s/he will be taught *See* **tshika, tshishkutamuakanu**

tshika tshissenitamuat they will know something *See* **tshika, tshissenitam**ᵘ

tshika ui atamishkuau you must give thanks to someone *See* **tshika, ui, atamishkueu**

tshika ui nakatuenitenan we must pay attention to something *See* **tshika, ui, nakatuenitam**ᵘ

tshika ui nashkumau you must give thanks to someone *See* **tshika, ui, nashkumeu**

tshika ui tshishpeuateiai we must defend something *See* **tshika, ui, tshishpeuatam**ᵘ

tshika uitsheutinau ma? can I come with you (pl)? *See* **tshika, uitsheueu, ma**

tshika uitshishpuminai you will eat with us *See* **tshika, uitshishpumeu**

tshika ut pakashtuepaniun you throw yourself into the water *See* **tshika, ut, pakashtuepaniu**

tshikamu VAI/VII it sticks, adheres, is attached

tshikamuniti/tshikamunitshi *See* **tshikamu**

tshikamunu *See* **tshikamu**

tshikaueu VAI s/he speaks loudly

tshikaueuat *See* **tshikaueu**

tshikutunnuepipuneshin you are ten years old *See* **tshi-, kutunnuepipuneshu**

tshimatakanit it is put up, erected *See* **tshimatakanu**

tshimatakanu VII it is stood up, erected, put up

tshimatan *See* **tshimatau**

tshimatau VAI s/he stands something up in place, puts something up

tshimateu VII it is put up, erected

tshimikaimᵘ VTI s/he chops, cuts something off with an axe

tshimikaueu VTA s/he cuts something (anim) with an axe

tshimushapu VAI s/he spies, watches secretly

tshimut P secretly, in secret

tshin PRO you

tshinameshim your fish *See* **tshi-, namesh**

tshinapishkat *See* **tshinapishkau**

tshinapishkau VII it (mineral) is pointed, sharp

tshinatutakunai s/he doesn't listen to us *See* **tshi-, natutueu**

tshinetshishepapatsh *See* **tshetshishepapan**

tshinishtipa P right away, immediately

tshipa PREV would

tshipa itinanapan something would happen *See* **tshipa, itu**

tshipa pimuteuatsh they would walk *See* **tshipa, pimuteu**

tshipa tshi pishtishuat they could cut themselves *See* **tshipa, tshi, pishtishu**

tshipa tshi pishtishuatsh they could cut themselves *See* **tshipa, tshi, pishtishu**

tshipa tutakaiaitsh it would be done *See* **tshipa, tutakanu**

tshipeikunnu-tatupipuneshin you are ten years old *See* **tshi-, peikunnu, tatupipuneshu**

tshipishkueu VTA s/he blocks the passage with the body or feet

tshishennu NA old person, elder

tshishennua *See* **tshishennu**

tshishennuat/tshishennuatsh *See* **tshishennu**

tshisheuepanu VII something makes a booming sound passing by

tshishe-utshimau NA government

tshishi- PREV finish

tshishipanu VAI/VII s/he, it goes fast

tshishitet *See* **tshishiteu**

tshishitetsh *See* **tshishiteu**

tshishiteu VII it is hot; it is hot weather

tshishi-utshimau-aiminanut *See* **tshishi-, utshimau-aiminanu**

tshishkutama(ti)shu VAI s/he practices by her/himself

tshishkutamatishuat/tshishkutamashuatsh they practice *See* **tshishkutama(ti)shu**

tshishkutamatishuht/tshishkutamashutsh *See* **tshishkutama(ti)shu**

tshishkutamuakanu VAI, PASS, s/he is taught

tshishkutamueu VTA s/he teaches someone something

tshishkutamut s/he teaches me

tshishpeuatam[u] VTI s/he defends something

tshishpeuateiai See **tshishpeuatam**[u]

tshishtapakun NA fir bough

tshishtapakunat See **tshishtapakun**

tshishtapakunit See **tshishtapakun**

tshishuaiku VAI, AG, IN s/he is made angry, irritated by something

tshishuapu VAI s/he is angry, mad

tshishunakushu VAI s/he is in a bad mood

tshissenimeu VTA s/he knows something about someone, something (anim)

tshissenitam[u] VTI s/he knows something

tshissenitamuat See **tshissenitam**[u]

tshissiumeu VTA s/he reminds someone

tshissiumiku See **tshissiumeu**

tshitapameu VTA s/he looks at, watches someone

tshitassi/tshitassin your land See **tshi-, assi/assin**

tshitassinan our (incl.) land See **tshi-, assi/assin**

tshitassinat/tshitassinatsh over our land See **tshi-, assi/assin**

tshitassinu our (incl.) land See **tshi-, assi/assin**

tshitinam[u] VTI s/he fetches something quickly

tshitineu VTA s/he fetches someone, something (anim) quickly

tshitishitatshimeu VTA s/he hauls someone away

tshitishitatshimimiht they haul us away See **tshitishitatshimeu**

tshititaiai we are here See **tshi-, tau**

tshitshinapunat NA milk; syn *tutushinapui*

tshitshineu VTA s/he fetches someone, something (anim) quickly; syn *tshitineu*

tshitshipaituat VAI, PL they leave together running or driving

tshitshipaituht See **tshitshipaituat**

tshitshipanituat VAI, PL they leave together running or driving; syn *tshitshipaituat*

tshitshipanitutsh See **tshitshipanituat**

tshitshitshinikunaiatsh they fetch us quickly See **tshi-, tshitshineu**

tshitshue P really

tshituss your aunt See **tshi-, utussa**

tshiueiat/tshiueiatsh we go back See **tshiueu**

tshiuetaieu VTA s/he takes someone, something (anim) home

tshiuetaik I bring it (anim) home See **tshiuetaieu**

tshiuetatshimeu VTA s/he drives someone back

tshiuetatshitsh we bring it (anim) home See **tshiuetaieu**

tshiueu VAI s/he goes, returns home

tshukumish your uncle See **tshi-, ukumisha**

U

u-, ut- PFX s/he, they, his/her, their

uaiu P far; syn *katak*[u]

uapam Look at it (anim)! See **uapameu**

uapamima Look at it (anim)! See **uapameu**

uapatinieu VTA s/he shows someone something

uapatiniueu VAI s/he, it (anim) shows, displays

uasheshkuianitsh See **uasheshkuiau**

uasheshkuiau/uasheshkunau VII it is blue

uasheshkunanit See **uasheshkunau**

uashkapuat/uashkapuatsh VAI they are sitting in a circle

uashteiapitiku VAI, AG, IN her/his eyes go white because of something (anim)

uepashtashun NI flag

uepashtashunnu See **uepashtashun**

uepashu VAI s/he, it (anim) is blown away

uepashuatsh they ar blown away See **uepashu**

uepinaman I cast See **uepinam**[u]

uepinam[u] s/he casts; syn *uepinam*[u]

uepinikusseu VAI s/he casts a fishing line

uet See **tshekuannu uet**

uetakussit that evening See **utakussu**

uetitshipanit/uetitshipanitsh See **utitshipanu**

uetshit See **utshiu**

ueuetak See **ueuetameu**

ueuetameu VTA s/he pulls someone out

ueuetatshimu VAI s/he crawls outside; syn *unuitatshimu*

ueuetimitsh P, LOC outdoors, outside (a dwelling); syn *unuitimit*

ueutshineu VTA s/he hugs someone, holds someone tightly in her/his arms

ueutshinit s/he holds me tightly in her/his arms
  See **ueutshineu**
ueutshipiteu VTA s/he hugs someone, holds someone
  tightly in her/his arms ·
ui PREV want to, tend to, have to, must
ui shutshishi be strong See **ui, shutshishiu**
ui uapatiniueu it (anim) must show something
  See **ui, uapatiniueu**
uiatshinanut *See* **uitshinanu**
uikanisha NAD her/his relative
uin PRO s/he, him, her
uinipunu VAI s/he, it (anim) runs
uinipunan I run *See* **ni-, uinipunu**
uinishtam PRO (to) her/him first
uinuau PRO they, them
uishameu VTA s/he invites someone
uitamuautsh *See* **uitamueu**
uitamueu VTA s/he tells someone something
uitamukau I tell them something
uitsh NID her/his house, tent, dwelling, home
uitsh *See* **tshekuannu uitsh**
uitsheuakaia/uitsheuakana NAD her/his friend
uitsheueu VTA s/he accompanies, goes with someone
uitsheutin *See* **uitsheueu**
uitsheutinau *See* **uitsheueu**
uitshi- PREV with
uitshimakuan VII it smells good
uitshimakushaueu/uitshimakushu VAI s/he, it (anim)
  smells good
uitshishpumeu VTA s/he eats with her/him
uitshishpuminai *See* **uitshishpumeu**
uitshinanu VII there is a house, a camp;
  people live there
uitshinatsh *See* **uitshu**
uitshinnua NAD her/his fellow Innu
uitshipatameu VTA s/he leaves with someone running
uitshitu VAI it (anim) is delicious, tastes good
uitshu VAI s/he has her/his house, tent somewhere
ukauia NAD her/his mother
ukaumau NA a mother
ukaumauat/ukaumauatsh mothers *See* **ukaumau**
ukauna NAD her/his mother; syn *ukauia*

ukuma NAD her/his grandmother
ukumisha NAD her/his uncle
ukutuan her/his fireplace See **u-, kutuan**
ume PRO, DEM this
unitshinikua NAD her/his relative, family; syn *uikanisha*
unuitaieu VTA s/he brings her/him outside
unuitaik I bring her/him outside See **unuitaieu**
unuitatshimu s/he crawls outside
upau VAI s/he flies, flies up
upauht/upautsh See **upau**
upuassimuaua her/his buses See **u-, puass**
upuassinu her/his bus See **u-, puass**
ushakamesh NI good place for fish
ushakameshimit See **ushakamesh**
ushameshet See **ushamesheu**
ushamesheu VAI s/he boils fish
ushkassikan NID her/his chest
ussinitshishkueu NA young woman
ussinitshishkueuatsh young women
  See **ussinitshishkueu**
ussinitshishu NA young man
ussinitshishuatsh young men See **ussinitshishu**
ussishikᵘ NID her/his eye
ussishikutsh in the eye See **ussishik**ᵘ
ut PREV from there, coming from
utakunishkueun her/his hat, cap
  See **u-, akunishkueun**
utakunishkueunit on her/his hat, cap
  See **u-, akunishkueun**
utakunishkueunitsh See **u-, akunishkueun**
utakunishkueun See **u-, akunishkueun**
utakussu VII it is evening, nightfall
utassi/utassin her/his land See **u-, assi/assin**
utat/utatsh P in the past
utauassimuaua their children See **u-, auass**
utauia NAD her/his father
utaumau NA a father
utaumauat fathers See **utaumau**
utaumauatsh fathers See **utaumau**
utauna NAD her/his father; syn *utauia*
ute VAI P, DEM here
utei/uten NID her/his heart

utin take it (anim) *See* **utineu**

utinakanit *See* **utinakanu**

utinakanu VAI, PASS s/he is taken

utinamᵘ VTI s/he takes something

utinamuk I take something of his *See* **utinam**ᵘ

utinatsh they take someone *See* **utineu**

utineu VTA s/he takes her/him, it (anim)

utishinikashunnu her/his name *See* **u-, ishinikashun**

utishinikashunuaua their names *See* **u-, ishinikashun**

utitshi/utitshin NID her/his hand

utitshipanu VII the time arrives

utshimau-aiminanu VII, IMPERS there is a meeting

utshipitaman I grab, seize something
   See **ni-, utshipitam**ᵘ

utshipitamᵘ VTI s/he grabs, seizes something

utshiu VAI s/he come from a certain place

utussa NAD her/his aunt

Designed by Veselina Tomova of Vis-à-Vis Graphics,
St. John's, Newfoundland and Labrador.
Printed in Canada.

ISBN: 978-1-927917244

Mamu Tshishkutamashutau Innu Education gratefully acknowledges funding support from
the New Paths for Education—Language and Culture Program of Indigenous and Northern Affairs Canada.

Running the Goat, Books & Broadsides is grateful to Newfoundland and Labrador's
Department of Tourism, Culture, Industry and Innovation for support through
the province's Publishers Assistance Program for our publishing activities.
We also acknowledge the support of the Canada Council for the Arts, which last year invested $153 million to bring
the arts to Canadians throughout the country.
Nous remercions le Conseil des arts du Canada de son soutien. L'an dernier, le Conseil a investi
153 millions de dollars pour mettre de l'art dans la vie des Canadiennes et des Canadiens de tout le pays.

Indigenous and
Northern Affairs Canada

Affaires autochtones
et du Nord Canada

Newfoundland
Labrador

Canada Council
for the Arts

Conseil des arts
du Canada

NUTAUI'S CAP is a co-publication from:

Running the Goat
Books & Broadsides
54 Cove Road / General Delivery
Tors Cove, Newfoundland & Labrador
A0A 4A0

www.runningthegoat.com

Mamu Tishishkutamashutau Innu Education
12 Edwards Drive
PO Box 539
Sheshatshiu, Newfoundland & Labrador
A0P 1M0

www.innueducation.ca